CROSSROADS AND BEYOND

A SELECTION OF POEMS BY

MAHMOOD MUSTAFA

Crossroads and Beyond
poems

Published by:
In Our Words Inc./inourwords.ca

Editor:
Cheryl Antao-Xavier

Creative Direction:
Anwar Mustafa

Layout Design:
Shirley Aguinaldo

Cover Image:
Luis Perdigao [UNSPLASH]

Author Photograph:
Nida Mustafa

Library and Archives Canada Cataloguing in Publication

Mustafa, Mahmood, author
Crossroads and beyond : poems / Mahmood Mustafa.

ISBN 978-1-926926-56-8 (paperback)

I. Title.

PS8626.U783C76 2015 C811›.6 C2015-906442-2

"I want to sing like the birds sing, not worrying about who hears or what they think."

RUMI

....

Dedicated to

THE BELOVED

....

ACKNOWLEDGEMENTS

Crossroads and Beyond is a humble effort to bring together a part of my poetic work to a wider audience.

Except for a small number of poems included here on the insistence of friends and well-wishers, the majority of them are new and have not been published before.

I would like to take this opportunity to thank each and every one of the individuals who have in some way or the other contributed to the compilation of this volume. First and foremost my thanks to my publishers In Our Words Inc. and their talented team, especially Cheryl Antao-Xavier for her editing, patience and faith in my work. My very special thanks to Professor Dr. Aqueil Ahmad for his warm, thought-provoking and highly intellectual foreword. Special thanks also to the renowned scholar, Professor Dr. Munir el-Kassem for taking the time to closely read and make suggestions on a portion of this selection. A very warm and heartfelt thank you to my son Anwar Mustafa for the exceptional cover and creative input in the design of this book, as well as my son Rafi Mustafa for being the first to read my manuscript and give it a professional nod. And last but not least, I would like to thank the two beautiful women in my life, my wife Nighath and my daughter Nida for their patience and encouragement all through these years! I hope you will read, enjoy, and if possible, pause to ponder on my thoughts and emotions, which were born in quiet solitude and are now being offered to the world.

The famous English poet William Wordsworth captured the essence of that poetic process when he wrote:

Poetry is the spontaneous overflow of powerful feelings: it takes its origin from emotion recollected in tranquility.

My hope is that these poems bring understanding and awareness of our common journey when we reach our own crossroads in life. I hope I succeed in this endeavour:

This presentation is not a collection of woes,
*I bring every piece after careful selection**

Mahmood Mustafa

* *Ye peshkash nahin majmooain parishani; Har aik cheze yahan intekhab layahun*
– Sikander Ali Wajd

CONTENTS

FOREWORD

....

By Dr. Aqueil Ahmad

In appreciation of Mahmood Mustafa's poems

It was about thirty-five years ago that I first came to know of Mahmood as a poet in addition to Mahmood, the man. And so it was about thirty-five years ago that I had the honour to read and comment upon his first collection of poems with a preface. That was a time when both of us were living in one of the most vibrant cultural centers in India, the city of Hyderabad. Then life changed for both of us, as it almost always does for most of us in a fast-changing world. In the middle of 1983, my family and I returned to the United States after an absence of ten years. And unbeknown to me, Mahmood migrated to Canada some years later. So we lost touch with each other, that is, until much later.

And so once again I have the privilege to read and comment upon another segment of his prolific poetry. I suppose it has been some time since Mahmood has penned his thoughts. He laments his poetic idleness for some time, the "dust on his table and cobwebs on his lamp," but is back at it with a vengeance and on a much wider canvas in "nurturing the pen and sleight," as the master Pakistani poet Faiz Ahmad Faiz would have it:

We shall continue to nurture the pen and the sleight;
*We shall continue to record how we bear and endure.**

Needless to say, I am as always much impressed not only by the breadth of his vision but by the depth of the emotions expressed. Art is always a reflection of the artist's own life, its past regrets and joys as well as its future fears, hopes and opportunities. Mahmood's work is not an exception. There is a touch of sadness about the past he left behind, his friends, parents and relatives. In that respect, Mahmood and I may be on the same page. That reminds me of an old Indian poet-friend, who once lamented:

....

* A rough translation of Faiz's countless masterpieces:
Hum parwarishe loh Qalam karte rahenge
Jo dil pe guzarti hai raqam karte rahenge.

I wish time could repeat old happiness and joys;
*I wish time would fly back the moments long past***

At the same time he also lets the reader into his journey to Canada as an immigrant and his love and respect for the adopted country, its open heart for the outsiders to become insiders, for the "aliens to become natives" with bountiful opportunities for all to share.

Mahmood's poetry is by and large also deeply spiritual. He extols the gifts and virtues of providential benevolence as well as the power of its Pen (the Qalam) that writes the destinies of men and materials on Earth, provides us with the beauty and bounties of nature, and gives us the wisdom of the ages through the words of wise men and messengers. Another Indian poet had once written that a poet is a link between humanity and eternity, meaning the Almighty. Mahmood's poetry definitely suggests that link as well.

Last but not the least, another striking feature of Mahmood's odes is their historical and cultural contexts, their awe and wonderment at nature and its boundless beauties and mysteries all the way from the deserts to green fields, from the roaring rivers to mighty mountains like the Himalayas. He exhorts his readers to appreciate their cultural heritage as well as admire and enjoy nature's boundless beauty that is not reserved for any peoples or groups. We are in it together.

Professor Dr Aqueil Ahmad is currently an adjunct faculty in the Department of Sociology at Elon University, North Carolina. He is also the Editor-in-Chief of Open Journal of Social Sciences. During the past quarter of a century he has served as a professor in the School of Management at Walden University, Minneapolis (2006 mid 2014) and sociology professor at the University of North Carolina Greensboro (1992 – 2006) and various other senior positions around the world.

** Rough translation of Nashur Wahidi's excellent original:
Ai kash usi eid ko doharata zamana;
guzre huey lamhat ura lata zamana.

Photo courtesy UNSPLASH

INACTIVITY

....

Cobwebs on my lamp...
A sure sign of inactivity!
And there is more proof:
The pen is thirsting for ink,
The paper, out of anticipation, is turning yellow,
The table is spread with dust
And the vase buried under withered roses.
So, I organize myself
Once again
And, with a disciplined finger,
Write in the dust ...
Poetry!

PRELUDE

....

Beginning in the Name:
Beneficence, Mercy;
All praise;
Cherishing, sustaining Worlds ...
Many known, hundreds obscure:
Unknown worlds,
Mysterious worlds,
Out there in the cosmos,
Buried below the crust,
Deep within the soul
Far into the mind,
Worlds behind worlds ...
Still, sustained and cherished
With grace and mercy!

Master, the only
Ruler, here, there and
On the Day
Judgment is pronounced:
Dossier upon dossier,
File over file,
Individual after individual,
Dealt with fairness
Dealt in truth
Dealt with accuracy,
Justice delivered
None denied!

The One adored
The One revered;
Sought for help,
Beseeched to grant
The straight path ...
The path of those
Bestowed with grace,
Saved from wrath,
Protected from straying!

THE NEW DAWN

....

Suddenly,
As I turned the corner,
A new dawn
With its hectic trade …
Advanced and marched
Straight into me;

And I, unprepared, unsteady
And still yawning,
Was run all over …
Totally overwhelmed;

Unprepared … for I was
Still battling
The hangover of an earlier day
… Its joys, its pleasures, its friends
And the haunts
So frequented even with eyes shut;

Unsteady … 'cause before I could
Shake off my lethargy,
Fully size it and
Come to terms …
Kind of grapple with it,
By the time I could find its horns
It had walked all over me,
Trampled me under its hasty feet;

And as I rose,
Clearing my eyes
Brushing off the dirt
And taking charge,
That new dawn was far into the horizon
With its hectic trade all around it,
It's back towards me ...
Now fading dust!

TIME*

....

And how the years rush by ... one big dash, the great blitz!
But on the sneak ... unnoticed, surging in silence!
The proof? The cradle, the youth, the silver, the stoop ...
A new-born town, a desolate city!

Time ... that subtle, uncompromising, unseen force,
Unconcerned, unattached, unforgiving and often unsympathetic,
The great reckoner ... bringing to book even the unconquered,
Laying low Romes and Babylons and Egypts in its wake.

Uncompromising – thinning the dense Amazonian forests,
Changing and shifting the course of many a mighty Nile,
Carving and reshaping the thundering Niagara, and
Thrusting up the Himalayas from the bowels of the Earth!

Unimpressed by the satin and gold of proud Persia,
Or horses and chariots of the haughty Pharaohs;
Unimpressed by the vastness of Alexander's domain
And unimpressed by the glint of Lionheart's sword.

Unstoppable in its flow – sweeping and swerving,
Time – that unbending, unseen, mysterious force,
In many respects the reflection of the *Master* Himself ...
From *then* to *then* – unquestioned, unchallenged!

....

* "Time" won the Editor's Choice Award and publication in The National Library of Poetry anthology, Maryland, USA.

THE SAGA OF MERGING

....

A short distance from the horizon ...
Far from the madding crowd
And very close to silence,
Almost *deafening* silence,
I sat and watched
Nature, Time, and Space
Play hide and seek!

The crimson of the sky,
The blue of the water and
The green of the fields,
Lent an admirable backdrop
To this huge saga of merging;

Though the hustle of returning seagulls
And the whistle of the wind in the trees
Momentarily shattered
The velvet calm
But then it was complete silence like before ...
Waiting for a pin to drop!

Somewhere between these hues and shades
An image peeped,
A ray glimmered,
A shadow lurked,
A cloak flowed,
A smile cracked and
A voice was heard ...
Life seemed to awaken and take flight
And from behind ...
A new dawn tumbled out!

THE AFTERMATH

....

Four wishes were granted,
Four – such abundance!
And I, so tired with life,
So disenchanted with the world,
Said: *Dawn be sudden,*
Eve be quick ...

A riot started heavenwards
– The fastest play of light and shade:
The stars went swishing by
Mad in a rush,
The sun, a fiery pendulum, sped to and fro,
And the moon was a peeled orange, scattered all over ...
The fastest play of light and shade!

Suddenly, I felt weak,
My weary feet ached,
Arms hung limp,
Back was a camel's hump,
And hair a silver mess!
Time had flown ... years had rolled by ...
Life had sped ... the past was dead.

I sat aghast
Seeing this shrunken frame,
I remembered the last two wishes
And said: *Dawn be slow,*
Eve relax ...

The storm died down
Life was normal like before,
The sun, the moon, the stars,
Fell back in rhythm,
But I cried aloud
For my youth was gone!

QALAM*

....

Before it begins to script,
A mandate is provided ...
Each word weighed
Each breath measured
Each moment planned:
It is then charged with inscribing destinies;

Unseen, unnoticed, inking fates,
Initiating conflicts and
Resolving them,
Appointing eras and
Spacing them
From flashes to eons;

Domains and realms designed,
Created and allowed
To grow, to thrive, to reach
Cosmic dimensions,
Spread further, spill over ...
And then slow down, and
Begin to reverse
Shrink and decay;

This *Qalam** is loaded,
The tip sharp
And the ink indelible,
And the Planner
Has it in His presence ...
At His command!

....

* An Arabic word for 'Pen.' In this context, the Eternal Qalam inscribing destinies

LET IT COME ALIVE

....

Let the fog clear
Let the sun shine ...
Brighter,
For it was always there
But only screened, hidden from view!

Let the path come alive
And throw its curves and bends
Far into the distance
Into the unknown horizon
To lands beyond view
To realms beyond imagination;

Let *cheer* rule again
And smiles blossom,
For we have washed our faces
Enough with tears ...
Although not a futile exercise
For it helped clear our vision!

Let love take over
Hand in hand with peace,
Let commotion retreat
Giving way to order,
Let justice spruce up
And preside!

TRULY, MAN IS IN LOSS

....

By the token of Time,
Through the Ages,
Without a doubt
Man is in loss;

By the passage of Time
As Day changes the guard
With Night,
Twelve full moons traverse the skies,
Decades, epochs on the march
Truly, Man is in loss;

Gloating over small triumphs
Bloating over minor victories
Boasting over petty wins
Blowing the trumpet out of tune
Bragging and dragging
His limited intelligence ...
Man surely is in loss

Sunk till the eyeballs in sins
Heavy-footed with faults,
One sharp eye on others
But the other turned blind on self,
Unconcerned about the past,
Ignorant, unaware of the beyond,
Man clearly is in loss;

The Nimrods, the titans couldn't last
Couldn't withstand, couldn't outsmart,
The sickle of time leveled
The mighty to the ground,
The robust to dust,
So where is the trivial?
Where are we?
Man indeed is in loss

Save those who believe,
Do virtuous deeds,
Follow and foster truth
Preach and practice patience!

THE BLESSED

....

The Eternal reflection,
The shadow of Forever,
The proof of the Unseen
The Last Word ... is You!

This earth, those heavens,
This light, that darkness,
Are Your different moods
Caught in the Spirit's infancy,
He made You –
And the rest is You!

We are sins,
You are mercy;
We are strife,
You are peace;
We are darkness,
You are light.

They frowned – You smiled,
They cursed – You forgave,
They hindered – You helped,
They stoned – You blessed!

Your name – a perpetual blessing,
Your thoughts – a pilgrimage,
Your teachings – the Holy Word
Your life – the religion you preached!

The secret of creation
Yet the knower of all secrets,
The mystery of Life
Yet the life of all mysteries
The unexplainable – is You,
Your example – is You!

CROSSROADS AND BEYOND

....

Standing at crossroads:
Unsure,
Hesitant,
Debating,
A little nervous,
A little apprehensive;

Which way
Is the right way ...
Which way
Is *the* way:
Hesitant,
Unsure,
Uncertain;

Standing at the edge
Markers to interpret,
Signs to read,
Milestones to measure
And a path to choose;
Crossroads and Beyond:
A bend, a bridge,
A fork ...
The unknown?

Photo courtesy UNSPLASH

WORDS

....

Empty words,
Shallow words, meaningless words:
Selfish, conceited, destructive ...
Used recklessly
Resulting in untold damage,
Broken hearts, distressed minds
Restless lives,
Shattering peace
Causing rifts,
Carving distances;

More words:
Empty, shallow, callous
Words,
Smacking of pride,
Dripping with affectation,
Insensitive to feeling;
Words simply to sound
Ego's trumpet;
Words to brag, to boast,
And at times bask
In glory that is stolen,
Is others;

And the antidote ...
The only antidote:
Wise, soothing words,
Kind, caring, thoughtful
And comforting words,

Spoken with concern and
Intent to help; to relieve, to alleviate,
Words changing attitudes,
Helping resolve conflict
Bringing hearts closer
Building bridges,
Shrinking distances:
Sincere words,
Gentle words
More *for* you
Than *of* me!

KUN*

....

From a meager heartbeat
To a major cataclysm;
From a weak whisper
To the mighty roar of thunder,
Hardly a moment passes
That the decree is not issued,
That the dictate is not active
That *Kun* is not being uttered
That *Kun* is not being heard!

From the minuscule iota
To the unfathomable expanses;
From the unkind harshness of reality
To the fluid metaphysics;
From the dense, ungraspable shadows
To the dazzling, unrivalled radiance,
Kun is scripting histories,
Kun is re-shaping geographies!

Marshalling and directing,
Creating, wiping out
And recreating
Just one word, one command
Kun –

So simple, so complete,
And by the same token
So real, so hallowed, so charged,
When uttered makes everything
Fall in place and
Find its purpose;
Kun, the Command, is perpetually working ...
Fully engaged!
When said *Be ....It Is!*

....
* A word in the Arabic language meaning "Be"

LAMHE*

....

Voices from the past,
Laughter, music, sighs,
Locked in the vault of Time,
Repeatedly echo – distantly heard
As the world spins
And an *age* passes;

Memory holds on to
Those moments, those faces, and those places
Fresh, young and near
As we have often remembered and wept;

Not one past *moment* is dead
It has only left centre-stage,
They are all there ... millions ... standing behind
The curtain of Time,
In the wings – waiting,

Waiting for the final command
And they shall be
Again what they used to be ...
A full life span re-lived

Right from the very first *sin*
Every drop squeezed out
Every second pulled back
Every empty canvas finding a face
And those *lost* and forgotten *'Lamhe'**

Again dancing on the brim of life
And what seemed dead
Being blessed with fresh breath!

And I shall stretch my hand
And snatch those moments,
And reclaim those voices,
Laughter and sighs
That I had lost on the eternal journey ...
My right, my souvenirs, my life!

....
* Urdu word meaning Moments

A WINDOW TO PEEK THROUGH

....

With so much lost
And countless departed,
Life shouldn't be anything
But a sad, sniveling story;

It is, in some ways,
But still ...
So *many* have been replaced
And so *much* has accrued
Substituting the *absent*,
The missing,
Giving life a purpose ...
... Making living a possibility
... A window to peep through,
With hope and joy
And looking to seize,
To capture
The past in the present!

THE LADY IN HIJAB*

....

The Mother ...
Full of grace, love and mercy;
Pure, protected, virgin ...
With charisma in name and presence,
A blessing for all times!

And we, the lost children,
Flock to her feet
... A Mother's feet ...
Where lies paradise
In all its splendor
With all its sparkle
With all its treasures
... Yet becoming insignificant, trivial
... At her feet
... A mother's feet!

Specially chosen,
Specially appointed
To carry and cradle
That 'singular miracle' ...
The Healer, The Comforter;
Mother! You are grace, you are love ...
You are pure, untouched,
You are the Lady in White
You are the Lady in Hijab*

* The Hijab refers to both the head-covering and modest style of dress, regardless of who wears it. In Arabic it means "to cover." There is nothing mysterious, sinister or hidden implied by the word.

NOOR[*]

....

Glowing bright
Like a *Lamp* in a *Niche*
Enclosed in a clean *Glass*,
The *Glass* shinning like a brilliant star
Lit with luminous oil
From the blessed *Olive Tree* ...
No fuel, no smoke, no waste ...
Light upon Light,
Filtering through the filigree
Of the universe ...
Everywhere,
Touching each soul, each object ...
A complete canvas of brilliance,
Spreading beyond imagination
Encompassing the highest ...
The lowest,
Giving life and sustaining it ...
Even past death;
Enlightening small minds,
Enlivening slumbering souls,
Enriching *existence* itself ...
Is the Eternal Light ...
The *Noor*,
Glorified again and again ...
The *Light* of the heavens and earth!

....
* An Arabic word for Light. In this context the Eternal Light.

Photo courtesy UNSPLASH

FROM BEHIND THE SHADOWS

....

Unseen, unknown, unfelt
There is so much going on
In all these empty spaces
In all the vacant lots;

The comings and the goings
The visitations, the recitations,
The invocations, the supplications
Not seen but transpiring;

From here to beyond
And from beyond to beyond,
A chain of events
Occurring each stacked minute;

Right under the nose
An unseen hand
Enters the throat
To pluck out another life;

Unseen, unknown, unfelt
There is so much going on
In spaces and lots
... Empty and vacant
Yet fully occupied!

INTROSPECTION

....

A day of joy and rebirth*;
Let the day of birth be
A day of reunion with self ...
A day of introspection,
A day of rediscovery;
Let there be a reflective pause
... A punctuation in life;
Fun, frolic, feast and flowers apart;
Time to measure, weigh and ponder
Time to evaluate and meditate
Time to deliberate and contemplate
A time to sit back and mull over:
How much has been achieved
How much remains to be accomplished
What is the pulse of *time* suggesting?
How far have we stuck to the agenda?
How far have we come in the long march?
Was the initial planning adequate?
A true time to assess, a true time to gauge
The aims, the goals, the ultimate!

....

* The commonly celebrated birthday where singing, feasting and gifts seem to mark the beginning and end of a year. A serious little introspection is sometimes needed!

GHALIB*

....

O Sage of the East, each word you said
Sinks deep in the mind and echoes long,
Those delicate thoughts that touched your head
Spill in melodious lyrics to bathe each song.

Your verse sublime encompassed all –
Love and life, heaven and earth,
Man and his virtues – his rise and fall,
His joys and sorrows, his birth, his death.

These falling tresses, those scarlet lips,
This broken heart, that wandering soul,
This silken veil that softly slips,
Two hands hold wine in a silver bowl!

Here love you lost, there bliss you found,
Here life deceived, there verse succeeded
The gurgling wine, the music and sound
You wisely to your verse did feed.

You gave to love your heart and soul
And earned in lieu a thousand tears,
Those tears in turn have changed to pearls
Which have sparkled your verse all these years.

An age has passed – an age indeed –
You left this scene, your pen caught rust,
But your verse still lives and that is your meed --
A living spirit though the frame is dust.

* Mirza Asadullah Baig Khan, or Ghalib as he was known, was one of the greatest Urdu and Persian poets of all times. Ghalib (1797-1869) lived in British India. He was the last great poet of the Mughal Era and his work remains popular to this day all around the world.

O CANADA!

....

I bring richness from the East
And add it to the wealth
Of my home and 'native' land:
O Canada, O Canada!
Our home and native land ...
The land of immigrants!

You have been a sanctuary,
A haven, a refuge
To the multitude,
To the millions,
To the clusters diverse
Who flock to you
For admission, for adoption
For settlement:
O Canada, O Canada!
Our home and native land
The land of immigrants!

Your arms open wide
To welcome and embrace
All cultures, all colors,
All creeds and all sects
Who sail to your shores
From numerous lands of the globe
Bringing in turn
Rich knowledge and wisdom,
Strengthening your stream
Of diversity and integration.

For many this is journeys' end
And for many more
You provide the launching pad
For future glories, for greater heights,
O Canada, O Canada!
Our home and native land
The land of immigrants!

May you ever prosper
May you always shine
May your fame spread far and wide
And may you remain the beacon
That you always were,
Guiding and welcoming new sons ...
Some broken, some shipwrecked,
Some robbed, some dejected ...
Who, once rejuvenated,
Will stand on guard for you;
O Canada, O Canada!
Our home and native land,
The land of proud immigrants!

LAKE COUCHICHING*

....

Breaking the mundane,
The run, the usual ...
Stepping out a little from the spotlight,
Finding a getaway
... Far from detection
And giving in to nature ... without fuss:
The essence of life ... a little life!
The essence of love ... a little self!

Lake Couchiching, in its serene majesty,
Its soft, lazy, sleepy waves,
Lapping the shores in rhythmic ripples,
The surrounding forests ... a canvas of bright patterns,
And the trees ... brushes of an artist ...
Stand dripping intense, fiery colors;
And autumn in its seasonal glory
Is in full bloom!

The morning breeze, with a slight nip
Adds freshness to the scene
And the new born sun
Lends brilliance to the surroundings,
And I, incidentally, stand silent and alone,
And witness
This rare kaleidoscope
And accept and count
One more free offering from Nature,
One more blessing added to the umpteen!

....

* Lake Couchiching is 16 km long and located in Central Ontario. It is separated from Lake Simcoe by a narrow channel where the city of Orillia is located. The lake is popular for fishing in summer and ice fishing in winter. In autumn, the trees in the area explode in unbelievably vibrant colours.

Photo: Mahmood Mustafa

THE STAFF

....

A piece of dead wood ...
Hard, cold and dry;
Used to lean on,
To fell leaves, to shepherd the herd;
To protect from lurking dangers;

That same piece of wood
Transforms to life,
Swells up with energy,
Finds movement and purpose,
Finds rhythm and verve and suddenly
Begins to hear and obey!

No deception,
No magic, no sham;
This is reality, this is truth;
And this truth in turn
Swallows up falsehood
Swallows up illusion;
Swallows up deception
Swallows up pompous pride;

The Staff knows its master,
Recognizes the touch
Falls in order
And makes believers
Out of heretics ...
This Staff performs 'The Act'
... Ushers in liberty!
This Staff attests to the piety
Of the Sage, the Prophet,
And his bright, shining hand!

RESOLUTION

....

And the price –
Emptiness!
Patience, Perseverance
The only remedies,
Prayer – the only comforter
And hope – the only shore.
Life has to be caught up with,
For it went ahead
As we stopped
To read the milestone!

A SIGN OF LIFE

....

Smoke ...
A sign of life ...
A suggestion that the fire
Is still burning;
That the spark is still glowing,
That the warmth is still emanating
That the light is still shining
That the senses are yet receptive,
That movement is still possible,
That the blood is still flowing;

And what else is smoke?
A sign that death is
Still at bay!

THE VISITATION

....

As I sat in my den
Grappling with issues
I heard a gentle knock and
Opened the door
And there to my amazement
Stood '*Time*'
In its patchwork attire of
Seasons and years;
Each *hand* held a mirror
Crystal and clear
Inviting me to explore
The veiled and obscure ...

The mirror in the left
Reflected the past
Stretching and fading
Into the beginning of *Time:*
The creation of space,
The evolution of stars
The growth of the universe
The shaping of the world;
Glimpses of history
From caves to castles,
From shields to shelters
From swords to guns,
From horses to jets,
From chariots to ships;
From kings to councils.

The mirror in the right
Projected the future
Racing through epochs
And melting into eternity,
Sweeping across cities
With brilliant neons
Rivaling the stars in nearby skies;
Skyscrapers with heads
In faraway clouds,
Men soaring into space,
Conducting commerce,
Extraterrestrials walking
In company of earthlings;
A wealth of knowledge
Available in abundance,
With information dancing
On fingertips and earlobes!

Then its eyes shone bright
And opened into windows
Displaying the present
A chilling sight:
Uncertainty, hunger, war and strife
Large sufferings, trivial prosperities
All around,
Whale swallowing fish,
Big brother robbing the small;
Nation warring nation
Color fighting color,
Creed throttling creed;
Bullies occupying territories;
Killings and murder – order of the day,
Human bombs exploding

In the name of religion;
In places of worship
In innocent marketplaces;
Lies, fraud and deception,
Camouflaged as leaders,
Misleading the helpless;

As I stood gazing,
Time paused,
Stepped in and slowly spoke:
"I visit mankind,
In varying shades –
Shades of good,
And shades of bad;
I even descend
Upon the mighty and pious,
For I am the reflection of Eternity;
And nothing is without purpose.
Call me not callous but bear with me,
Value me, treasure me, and honor me
For I bring both pain and peace
And once I depart
I seldom return,
And then ...
I am also depicted as 'opportunity':
For I knock at least once
On each individual door:
"Hear me, respond and you have seized the moment;
Neglect, ignore and you have lost a lifetime!"

ROLES

....

"All the world's a stage, and all the men and women merely players;" — William Shakespeare

In one life,
In one small world
On one individual stage ....
Enacting many roles
At the same time
In the same breath,
Is a man:

He is the loving husband
The providing father
The obedient son
The trusted friend
The tough yet caring boss
The hardworking staff
The faithful and brave brother
And when age catches up
In this unnoticed race
Turning him quite 'majestic,'
He assumes a new role
That of the grand patriarch ...
The doting grandfather ...
The cycle seems complete,
The grandfather begins
Seeing himself in the child ...
And effortlessly starts
Receding into infancy:
'Sans teeth, sans eyes, sans taste, sans everything'!

BREATH IN CLAY

....

Life ... I have often sat and mused
Why was it placed in clay?
Why blood and flesh were fused?
Why this heart was made to play?
Was it to reach the stars and moon?
To make the heavens sway,
To cloud the burning noon
To light the night like day,
To conquer time and speed
To fly the spreading blue
To make the oceans plead
To scatter the old for new,
But how does this capture death?
For life has soon to roll,
But was it to house another soul
This clay was freed from breath?

THE WINTER CHARM

....

Soft snowflakes, like petals,
Descend silently
On land and lake,
Thickening the already laden layers
Polishing what was polished before;
The trees, with their silver branches,
Like the locks of a *fakir**,
Move with the breeze, thoughtfully,
And the trunks, snow-bit, stand limp.

The whole town
Spreads like a fairyland
With snow-topped roofs
Chimneys exhaling lazy plumes of smoke;
Snow meets the eye
As far as the vision stretches
And the distance fades in one fluffy hue!

This splendor so rare
Turns the *slumbering within*
Into a stormy ocean
Silent to the lips
Rises a single prayer ...
"God bless poetry"!

....

* Fakir = Sage, Holy man

FOOTPRINTS IN STONE

....

For all times ... for all ages ...
Footprints left in stone
By men of stature, men of greatness,
Men of purpose, men of distinction.

Striking a path ... a different path,
The right path ...
A path of truth, sincerity, courage,
The path of virtue ... path so original
A path to be emulated ...
For all times, for all ages
Footprints left in stone;

Permanent footprints,
Exemplary footprints,
Footprints reminding sacrifice,
Echoing hardships,
Ringing devotion, showing toil
Depicting steadfastness
Reliving history ...
From the first footprints
At Adam's Peak
To footprints in the Holy Lands ...
Journey from heaven to earth
And journey the other way around ...
Sacred footprints!

Footprints from the East
To footprints in the West ...
Footprints for all times
Left in stone!

THE PINNACLE

....

What when you have the absolute power
To execute the impossible,
What when you have mastery over
All the conceivable sciences,
Coupled with command of all known
And unknown languages;
And you are the finest artist of all times;
When you compose rhythm to the ultimate note
When you construct and erect the most unique
And robust structures;

What when you can paint the night its original black
And the day authentic white
What when you possess the capacity to color
Forest after forest in myriad shades of green,
And can fill oceans, rivers and lakes
With varying tones of blue,
When you can raise a massive canopy
Without support, without pillars
And create beings that glide through the air
Without any supplementary help;

What when you can move a cloud and squeeze
Rain out of it
And blow the wind and
Generate a massive storm;
When you can perform feats that others
Can't even conceive,
When your intellect, brilliance and innovation

Begin where everybody else's is spent
Or has reached the ceiling
When you can envision a *phenomenon*
And it *becomes;*
Then you are at the pinnacle of power and more
Then You are Him, the Creator!
Yes, it is You ... the Creator!

THE THRESHOLD

....

Waiting on your threshold
With years as witnesses on my side ...
Waiting for recognition,
For attention,
For love!
Distractions,
Diversions
And temptations
Occurring
All around ...
Calling,
Luring
Enticing ...
Trying to suck and trap
Yet the flame lit within
Keeps burning.

The raging passion is
Still unflinchingly loyal
And the needle
Unyieldingly devoted,
Still true
Still pointing north;
Waiting on your threshold
For a glance,
A smile,
A nod,
For that face ...
An eternity sold
An eternity bought!

FREEDOM

....

Soft melting ocean clouds
Multi-hued,
Scattered at small distances,
And the sky,
Like a scarlet ribbon,
Stretches ...
From where spring
Varying colors in rapid succession
All from the west to the east!

The distant mountains
– Rising unobstructed
– Laden with perpetual snow,
Work as a mirror and
Reflect back rainbows ...
One set after another!

And this valley,
Fresh from recent showers,
Spreads luxuriously,
Green and ochre fields
Dance lightly in the soft breeze
Emitting fragrance
Of wet wood and shrub;

Freedom ...
O glorious freedom ...
Live long!

PIR PANJAL*

……………………………

I can almost hear you
Whisper those mysterious tones
Hushed in a silent stir
As the wind softly blows,
You at such a distance
White, and as the sun sinks
Go pink … as though a blush,
The canvas behind you inks
To a darker shade … almost dense;

And I can almost smell
The pines and poplars in your valleys
Breathing fresh, the wet branches
Swinging with the dancing wind
Throwing a thousand rays
Aimlessly all about,
The pathways damp with recent rain
Not fully wet but not dried as yet;

And in the west the sun
… A red hot disc …
Slips over the land
Coating the east a little brighter
For one last time … anew;
Golden, purple clouds
Scattered at lonesome distances
Seem to shudder with the sudden
Chill, and rapidly cover

Themselves in darker cloaks
And you turn distant and dark
Slowly turning grey
Or hardly grey ... colorless,
Melting in that forlorn horizon;

The land and sky look one ...
Dark, the end of a majestic eve,
But a last whisper from you
Reaches me, almost like a secret,
"Darkness and existence were never related,
Wait for the sun
And you shall see me
Much brighter ... much stronger"!

Courtesy Wikipedia https://commons.wikimedia.org/wiki/File:KashmirVale.jpg

* A range of mountains that lie in the Inner Himalayan region and run across the Indian state of Jammu and Kashmir

SHED A TEAR

....

How can one be human
And not shed a tear?
All you beings of 'iron and steel'
Learn to weep
Lest you catch rust!

Learn to shed tears,
Learn to live,
Learn to melt,
Perpetually doling out agony
At times suffer and grow;
A few dents, a few bruises
Will hurt a little
And in turn will offer
The sense of pain,
Which will help you
Understand sorrow
And will add value,
Appreciation,
To the joys in life!

MYOPIC

....

Living in silos
Not thinking beyond,
I always in focus
Not a thought for *them*;

A life of shadows,
Uncertain, unsure goals
And believing this
To be reality;

Presumptions, conjectures,
Conclusions, fixations ...
Small minds, small flights,
Small hearts, small offerings;

Living in silos
'Now' is the ultimate,
Living in silos
Not seeing beyond the eyelid!

THEN AND NOW

....

The night was long, peaceful,
Only at times scary,
And the moment my eyes closed
The day ended for good,
Save a few isolated dreams
That would find their way
But would wait till dawn
To remind me of a bygone day …
My comfort, my security
Was that huge bed
Wherein I would lie to feel safe,
To rest and meet the sun
With new energy and joy …
But that was *then*!

The night is still long
Or maybe longer still!
But there is no peace,
Neither is it scary
For the day is filled
With much more horror,
The bed has shrunk too
And with it comfort and security,
Wherein I sit to watch the sun
Rise and spread its too challenging light,

Maybe the spark within is dead …
Maybe the child has walked out on the house …

LET THERE BE LIGHT

....

Let those opaque windows
Open and
Let the light
Pour in;

Let those thickly curtained,
Suffocated minds
Breathe ...
They need to live,
Open their eyes
And step out of darkness,
Denseness and see,
Become aware,
Find purpose, get enlightened
And contribute;
Shake off the dust
Of prejudice, bias, ignorance
And chauvinism;
Let those windows open,
Let there be light!

THE CARAVAN MOVES ON

....

And the caravan moves on ...
How brief was the camp
How short was the stay;
We had just pitched the tent
Begun collecting wood for the fire
And water for the jar,
Commenced preparing the meal
Letting all the fragrances
And essence
Drift and go wild ...
We thought we will rest a while,
Maybe dig ourselves
In for a longer tenure,
Maybe find roots
Settle and spread,
But no ...
The 'Keeper' blows the whistle
Proclaiming the 'end of time',
No option to linger,
No excuse to delay,
Hardly a chance to pack,
Must retreat –
Must quit ...
For the caravan has to move on!

THE CHINAR* HAS DISAPPEARED

The Chinar* has disappeared away in the past,
The canker has feasted upon the rose,
The cuckoo has flown with a tired glance
All joy is sunk, there is no repose;
The meadows have lost their silky green
The trees are a shame to look upon,
The playful stream is wanting and thin
And crying silence spreads around
The moon is an ugly patch of pale,
The sun, a source of blurred light,
Heaviness hangs from vale to vale,
And no peace offers the cherished night.

* The Chinar is a popular tree in Kashmir (India). It has broad, thick leaves that tend to orient horizontally. The tree is valued for its shade during the hot season. The majestic Chinar is ubiquitous in scenic Kashmir and in its cultural lore. Its leaves fall in November and new leaves appear in April. In autumn, the Chinar trees are spectacular in colour, similar to Canada's maple tree.

OCEAN YEARNING

....

To my ears there comes the sound
Of softly rolling ocean waves,
With a thousand gulls hustling around
Resounding echoes from distant caves.

I listen to them in solitude
And silently yearn to rejoin
The company that once I viewed
Now left far, far behind.

The ocean stretched along the sky
To lands beyond this human eye,
The foaming waves rising high
Sent a whistle – the ocean's sigh!

A million tears its bosom had
Yet smiling powerfully it rolled on,
It endured both – good and bad
Although at times it seemed forlorn.

Oh! How I wish I could be again
In the company of the ocean dear
Which gave me strength, reduced my pain
And taught my eye to shed a tear!

THE BEACON

....

Your thoughts are a shelter,
A refuge
From the cold, callous, piercing
Winds of change ...
From the unkind world;

Your words are solace
Hearing them
Repeating them ...
We take heart;

Your name is the beacon
That keeps the direction straight
Through the fog of uncertainty
Like a compass
Guiding on to the right course
Keeping the head high
... Looking up, looking *North*, looking forward;

And this home is your *abode*
To be adored and loved ...
The nucleus,
An ocean without shores
Of love, compassion and mercy
You, the Friend, the Guide, the Mentor!

THE LAST WORD

....

Remembrance, unscathed,
Lived,
The rest crumbled
Under the yoke of time;

Remembrance – one word
But so potent:
A request
A plea
A call
To keep the past,
That glorious sensation,
Living in the future;

Remembrance –
The last word,
The last look,
The last touch,
The last embrace,
Yet foremost
In the annals of memory!

ABOUT THE POET

....

Mahmood Mustafa

Mahmood Mustafa immigrated to Canada in 1993 from Dubai, in the United Arab Emirates. He graduated from the prestigious Osmania University in Hyderabad, India, with a focus on English literature. He then lived briefly in England before returning to India to pursue a career in journalism. Mahmood also worked as a journalist at Khaleej Times in Dubai and has freelanced in Canada.

He continued to be an avid reader of English, Urdu, and Hindi literature. His extensive travel around the world has influenced the style and theme of his work. His poetry forms a literary canvas influenced by the complex hues of his study of philosophy, mysticism, and history. Mahmood published two collections of poems in India. Crossroads and Beyond is his first collection published in Canada. He lives in Whitby, Ontario, with his wife and three children and works as Manager, Settlement Services, with the Community Development Council Durham.

www.ingramcontent.com/pod-product-compliance
Ingram Content Group UK Ltd.
Pitfield, Milton Keynes, MK11 3LW, UK
UKHW020138250726
13967UKWH00002B/723